LIFESTYLE REDESIGNED

Banishing 7 Hidden Wastes from Your Life to Make Room for What Matters Most

Yvetta Varatharaj

LIFESTYLE REDESIGNED: BANISHING 7 HIDDEN WASTES FROM YOUR LIFE TO MAKE ROOM FOR WHAT MATTERS MOST

This book is dedicated to my family, all the A. J. V.s in my life. You are the reason this book needed to exist. I don't want a single minute with you to go to waste! To my husband who supported me through this project (and would occasionally remind me that he always knew I was going to write a book), thank you for believing in me. To my kids, may you always pursue the most important things in life, which aren't things at all.

To my mom, the queen of tidiness and efficiency, thank you for setting an example for me. To Mom V, Abisha, and Bethany, the three beautifully different minds who each helped me polish up this manuscript, you challenged me to think outside the box and I am so glad you did!

Lastly, I dedicate this book to God, the one with whom all things are possible.

Contents

Preface.. 6

1. Domestic Engineering: An Introduction................. 7

2. Value 13

3. Waste 24

4. Organization... 31

5. Visual Cues 46

6. Gaining Skills 54

7. Flow and the Experience of Work.................... 61

8. Using the Tools.. 72

9. Toolbox and Launchpad 84

10. Big Picture Domestic Engineering.................... 89

11. A Culture of Improvement 94

    Appendix 103

    Bibliography 116

In a not so distant past life, I worked as an engineer and technical writer who was keen on hunting for ways to make processes better in the workplace. In those years I was being trained on principles of Lean Process Management, leadership, and other topics that would set me up for a successful future in the corporate world. I soon found myself applying these very relevant management principles to the processes I encountered in my life outside the workplace as well. I would pay attention to traffic patterns during different times of the day to find the quickest path on the routes I drove frequently. I would analyze the way I prepared dinner to see if I could cut out steps without sacrificing the final product. I'd try new ways of doing things to see if I could do them better than before. I was continuously fine-tuning things, because I knew there was always the possibility of finding a better and less wasteful method, no matter the task.

When I became a mom and decided to spend these precious years at home raising our little world-changers, I began to understand that my new job of managing my home was not something that would just happen accidentally. If it was truly worth me giving up a corporate job (as I knew it was), I'd better take my new roles and responsibilities pretty seriously. In this quest to be the best mom and home manager I could be, I found myself constantly learning and improving my ways of doing things. I began to blog on these improvements and other ideas at www.more-than-rubies.com. This book is a result of me, the manager of my home, looking at life through the eyes of an engineer, lean thinker, and continuous process improver.

1

Domestic Engineering: An Introduction

Imagine you are the owner and operator of a small but dynamic company producing a wide range of goods and services. Some of your job responsibilities include running and maintaining equipment, managing inventory, supporting the needs of your employees, taking orders from customers, and fulfilling those orders. Sounds like a pretty important job, doesn't it?

If you agree, I hope you also feel that same sense of importance when you think of managing your own home. Do you see the similarities to the company I just described? Your home is like a corporation, with you at the top. You manage day to day operations on the home front. You handle the logistics of daily tasks and carry them out. You create the environment and culture. You anticipate and serve the needs of your family members and others you are responsible to outside the home. You shop for the goods your household uses. You work hard to keep tasks running smoothly so those who depend on you always have exactly what they need, when they need it.

Are you following?

If you can see the parallels between a home and a company, you won't have a hard time believing me when I tell you that some of the methods used by corporations to improve their systems can actually help you run your home more smoothly as well. On the home front, the goal is more efficient use of your time and resources, less stress for you and your family, and a better-functioning home environment. The result is a bigger capacity for what you love in your life and less of what you do purely out of necessity.

Benefits

A system called "lean" has been helping companies become better and faster at what they do, and to accomplish their mission with less errors and waste since the concept was first introduced in the early 1990's. Lean companies have been able to do more with less, and serve their customers' needs more effectively. It has resulted in less inventory and storage space for the companies, and a faster turnaround time for orders. Lean companies have happier employees who are more invested in their work. It has created corporate cultures that seek to continuously "up their game," with perfection as the ultimate, but unattainable, goal.[1]

------

[1] James P. Womack and Daniel T. Jones, *Lean Thinking: Banish Waste and Create Wealth in Your Corporation* (New York: Free Press, 2003).

A book called *The Machine that Changed the World* was the first to define this concept.[2] It describes revolutionary manufacturing strategies that the car manufacturer Toyota had implemented in the years after World War II with great success. Womack and Jones later published *Lean Thinking* which made these wildly successful lean principles accessible to the masses.

This book you are holding now reframes many of the concepts of lean laid out by Womack and Jones, and applies them to an entirely different type of system: the home. While doing this, it also includes other relevant strategies for creating the home life you desire that are not found in any lean book. This book is unique from other home management books in that it doesn't tell you how to run your home. Instead, it empowers you, dear reader, to re-engineer your life how it makes sense to you and your family. This is what I call "Domestic Engineering".

Lean in the Home

As you read this book, you will re-design your home life to allow more time, space and resources for what you and your family value most by applying lean principles to the things you do every day. In the coming chapters you will learn to apply these game-changing principles to every process you encounter, making room for what you actually want, value, and seek to accomplish. When you see the tasks in your home through the lens of value, you can engineer each one to serve your family better while minimizing waste.

---

[2] James P. Womack, Daniel T. Jones, and Daniel Roos, *The Machine That Changed the World: the Story of Lean Production - Toyotas Secret Weapon in the Global Car Wars That Is Revolutionizing World Industry* (London: Simon & Schuster, 2007).

Waste is anything that doesn't add value to you and those you serve, whether in the form of unnecessary steps, storage, movement from one place to another, or waiting for things to finish before you can move on. When you remove the waste in all its various forms, you hone in on the things your family really values and free up your time, energy, and resources from the things that just have to get done.

Real World Examples

Would you like to see how this way of thinking has worked for me? Here are a few examples.

- I have revamped the way I do grocery shopping, getting in and out faster with small kids in tow, eliminating a 90 minute trip every other week, and reducing the amount of food that gets wasted.
- I have "hacked" my favorite recipes by reducing the amount of dishes, time, and effort involved, and improved the consistency and quality of the finished product through studying and improving the processes.
- I have successfully taken on the task of preparing for and hosting large gatherings at my house, even with three small kids at home.
- I have managed to get some time to myself nearly every day, even with three small children in my care.
- I have made packing for trips into a science that works for my family and minimizes the time we spend rummaging through the suitcase at our destination
- I have decluttered my clothing storage areas, purged about half of my clothes, and organized everything in a way that fits how I use it. I now spend less time deciding what to wear.

- I have filled my schedule with activities my family finds valuable and minimized the time and effort spent on tasks which are necessary but not enjoyable to me.

Do these results sound exciting to you? This book is your manual and workbook to allow you to re-design each task and process in your home to have less waste, so that what's left is what actually adds value to your life.

Key Concepts

There are a couple of concepts that will provide the foundation upon which you will use lean principles to redesign your home and life.

Customer- Your customers are the people and groups you serve, including yourself, your family, work outside the home, friends, and social groups. These are the people you are responsible to; they expect things from you.

Value- What your customers actually want, need, and expect from you. Value has little to do with what *you* are good at or what *your* capabilities are. It is defined by the customer. What do these people and groups you serve *actually* want from you?

7 Wastes

Steps that don't create value in a process are waste. Lean identifies waste in seven different forms, all of which use up our precious time and resources, and limit our capacity to keep up with the things that are actually valuable to us and those we serve. Here is an overview of them. You will run across them in many places throughout the book because they are the heart and backbone of lean.

Overproduction- Producing things before they are needed.

Transport- Movement of materials.

Movement- Movement of people.

Over-processing- Complicating things with extra steps.

Waiting- Not being able to move to the next step.

Inventory- Storing more than the minimum.

Defects- Things that aren't done right and must be redone.

Can you think of some examples of waste as you read these? As these seven types of waste become ingrained in your thinking, you will start seeing waste everywhere as you go about your daily routines. You'll look at a process you've been doing one way for years, have an "aha" moment, make a minor tweak, and suddenly it becomes easier, simpler, and faster.

The idea here is that if it doesn't directly add value to the people benefitting from the task, then it's waste. If we know what is actually needed by the person we're performing a task for, then we can redesign the process to get rid of steps that don't add value to them.

Perfection

What does perfection mean to you? You might have heard the phrase, "perfection isn't the point." Here's the truth about perfection. There is always something to improve. If you ever feel like you've achieved perfection, then you've given up on improving. Perfection isn't a status you can achieve in your home or life. This is one reason you will not see this book telling you "perfect" ways of doing the tasks you must accomplish every day. The most perfect way of doing something is the way that maximizes value for *you* and those you serve. No matter how ingeniously designed a process may seem, if it's not doing exactly what you need it to do, no more no less, then it's not the best– keep perfecting it.

2

Value

How do we figure out what really adds value to our lives? Why is value important?

Customers

In order to define what's valuable in our lives, we have to start by knowing whom we serve. Businesses thrive when they know who their customer is and can serve their specific needs. If your home and life were a business, who would be your customers?

This is a loaded question but I'll break it down into a few different categories so you can pinpoint these people in your own life. The first people you are responsible to are your immediate family members, roommates, and/or any extended family members in your care. Note them here:

____

____

____

You would probably agree that serving their needs is your primary responsibility.

The next category encompasses parties and groups outside your home with whom you are involved. List any work, social groups, church, committees, community groups, and hobby groups here:

____

____

____

Think of these people and groups as your regular customers. You may occasionally have other projects that come up that serve different people, and the same principles in this manual can be applied to those as well.

Value

Now that you know who your customers are, you can ask yourself, "What do each of these people actually value, desire, or expect from me on a day to day basis?" The focus here is on them and their needs, not on you and your skills and abilities. If you are providing your customers with goods or services, what would be the ones they actually need and want from you? We will go deeper on this later on, but start thinking about this question.

If your goal is to focus your efforts on the things that are important and cut down on the time and energy you spend on things that don't really matter, it is important to first figure out what that important stuff is to you and those you serve.

Let's start with family. I will use my own family as an example.

We *all* value:

- time together as a family,
- a clean home,
- healthy meals,
- clean clothes,
- outside adventures,
- hosting others in our home,
- thoughtful and respectful relationships, and
- opportunities to serve others.

I value:

- time to myself to read, pray, and journal;
- outings with other moms; and
- an organized schedule.

My husband values:

- support from the home front so he can focus on work,
- time to pursue his hobbies, and
- homemade Indian food.

My kids value (or need):

- attention,
- training/education,
- naps,
- playtime,
- social time,
- exploration,
- outings,
- outdoor play,
- reading,
- emotional and physical nurturing,
- protection,
- spiritual upbringing,
- intellectual stimulation, and

- conversation.

How about you? Let's go back to those you listed earlier. What do those closest to you need and expect from you?

People:	What they need and expect from you:

What about the outside groups/entities we are responsible to?

For me, my Bible study group expects and values certain things from me. These include: preparing for our lessons, leadership, a positive role model, transparency, relationship, a sense of community, etc.

Now it's your turn. For each of those outside people or groups you listed earlier, what do they expect or need from you?

Outside person or group:	What they need and expect from you:

The things you've started jotting down in this section are the things that actually add value to your life or to the lives of others you serve.

Now that you have defined what you should be focusing your efforts on, this list is your plumb line. When you break down processes in your quest to eliminate waste, every step will fall into one of three categories relative to what you outlined just now. It either adds value to the customer, doesn't add value to the customer and is unnecessary to the process, or doesn't add value but *is* necessary at this point in time.

If you are finding yourself resistant to this process, I want to point something out to you. In some cases you may find that steps that add value in a process are not necessarily the most efficient way to achieve the finished product. Do not remove them simply because they take unnecessary time or complexity if they add to your overall quality of life. If making your mom's ravioli recipe from scratch with twenty five different steps reminds you of precious moments you spent with your mom in your childhood, don't try to make it more efficient. You will be short-changing yourself and actually removing what makes the process valuable to you. That being said, there are many processes we do day to day that could be improved without sacrificing our enjoyment of them or our quality of life.

Pick one of the expectations listed above for which you can easily see a clear-cut process. Would you like to improve your efficiency on it using the lean method? The first thing we are going to do is break the process down into individual steps, from start to finish.

We will look at a laundry process. Do you dread this chore as much as I do? Let's see how we can improve it.

Jim throws his laundry on the floor in the bathroom where he gets dressed. When it piles up, he moves the piles into the hamper in the bedroom. Then, about once a week he takes the hamper to the laundry room and sorts it. He does a load of light colors first, which may not be full, but since he already carried it over there he might as well wash it. Then he transfers it to the dryer. He discovers one of his shirts has a stubborn stain that didn't get clean, so he puts it back in the hamper to spot treat for next time. After the dryer is done, he puts it all in another hamper and carries it to the living room where he folds and sorts everything. He then carries one stack to the kitchen, one to the linen closet next to the laundry room, and one stack to his bedroom closet. He puts them away until the next time he wears them.

Can you tell that there is waste in Jim's process? Jim reads this book and starts to see some waste in how he does his laundry so he makes a few improvements.

Let's outline the process in list form:
- Throw dirty clothes on bathroom floor as he takes them off.

- Put dirty clothes into hamper in bedroom.
- Carry hamper to laundry room.
- Sort lights and darks.
- Place one load into washer, whether full or not.
- Add detergent and oxygen booster.
- Run wash load.
- Transfer to dryer.
- Run dryer.
- Set aside stained shirt for rewash at a later date.
- Place second load into washer.
- Add detergent and oxygen booster.
- Empty dryer.
- Transfer 2nd load to dryer.
- Carry Load #1 to living room for folding.
- Carry Load #2 to living room for folding.
- Fold clothes, towels, and sheets.
- Sort by type.
- Deliver piles to respective locations around the house.

The steps we want to keep are those that actually provide value toward our end goals. In the laundry example, these would be things like washing and drying, folding or hanging the clothes, and putting them away. If the goal is to have clean clothes in the closet, all of these steps directly add value to Jim and the people he serves with this task.

The steps that don't add value at all and could easily be cut out are picking up clothes from the floor, emptying the clothes from the dryer to a large laundry bag, and carrying the clothes to the living room for folding. These steps are obvious waste in the form of over-processing, motion, and transport. This is some low-hanging fruit in Jim's quest to reduce waste.

Jim has been doing it this way because the washer and dryer have clutter on top. If he removes the clutter he can do the folding there instead of having piles of laundry on the couch.

For the most part, the other steps are necessary, though they don't add value to the family. These are also brimming with potential as far as reducing waste is concerned.

Here is how Jim re-engineers his laundry routine. He decides to move the hamper into his master bathroom. He starts to notice that his floors are less cluttered because he puts the clothes directly in the hamper. Next, he realizes that the sorting is an unnecessary step - though he needs to have clothes separated by color, he figures out that having two hampers can cut out the sorting step for him because he can throw the clothes in the right bin as he takes them off. This setup also allows him to see when one hamper is getting full, indicating that it's ready to be washed as a full load. He uses a clothespin to attach things requiring spot treatment onto the side of the hamper so he can avoid having to wash them twice. After the load goes through the washer and dryer, he pulls out the big, bulky towels and sheets and folds and puts them away immediately in the adjacent linen closet. He cleaned off the top of his dryer so that he can fold clothes there and save a trip to and from the living room. When he's done folding, he can now take each of the remaining piles straight to where it needs to go. Jim has eliminated several unnecessary steps from his laundry routine, and now he gets it done quicker overall, and there isn't a mess of clothes in the bathroom and living room. The result is that it takes him less time to do it, and he can wash loads less frequently because he knows when he has a full, sorted load ready to go.

Here is how the process looks now:

- Place worn clothes into light and dark hampers.
- Clip items with stains to the side of hamper.
- When full, carry a hamper to laundry room.
- Spot treat if necessary.
- Put clothes in washer.
- Add detergent and oxygen booster.
- Run washer.
- Transfer clothes from washer to dryer.
- Set dryer settings.
- Run dryer.
- Pull out towels and sheets first and fold.
- Put away towels and sheets in adjacent linen closet.
- Fold other clothes on top of dryer.
- Place into appropriate piles for each room while folding.
- Deliver to correct rooms and closets.

Can you see how small changes to the process can make a noticeable difference? Jim started by assessing where the value was in the process, then hunted for steps that didn't add value. He made a few minor tweaks that resulted in a noticeable payoff of less mess, less re-washing, less carrying clothes around the house, and less loads to do altogether. That is quite an improvement!

3

There is only one of you. You are an amazing person, but there are only 24 hours in the day, and we've already established that there are many things you value and would like to be doing with that time. There are also limits to your finances, the space in your home,

your resources, etc. Are you content with how you currently use your time and resources, and the things you are able to accomplish in the day?

When you learn to identify waste you are able to start removing it. You are the expert of your own routines and habits, and the processes in your home. But being in a position where you have been doing something the same way for weeks, months, or years can make you blind to alternative (read: better) ways of doing things.

What if I could give you a new pair of glasses to look through? You are going to look at the things you do often and see them in a different way. Now that you've thought about what you value, it is time to learn what waste really is. Waste is something that uses resources without adding value. You don't need that in your life!

Rework

Rework is doing things more than once because they weren't done correctly the first time.

Examples:

- You assemble a PB&J sandwich for your kid, and then he tells you he can't take peanut butter to school because a child in his class has an allergy, so you make him a new sandwich.
- You run the dishwasher and don't unload it, and the next person doesn't see it marked clean, so they put an ice cream bowl in there and it drips onto the other dishes. You run the load again because you don't know what's clean.
- Your spouse offers to pick up diapers from the store, but guesses the wrong size and gets ones which are too small. They have to be exchanged.
- You fold socks for your kids but then they unfold them and make a ball out of them before putting them away.

Overproduction

Overproduction is the production of items not needed or ahead of demand.

Examples:

- You make a meal with so many leftovers that you can't finish them before they go bad.
- You make goodie bags for a party before you have the RSVPs, and end up with lots of extras.
- You pre-make lots of frozen breakfast burritos for your spouse to take to work, and then your spouse tells you he/she is starting a cleanse diet and will be eating only fruits and veggies for a while. You won't be able to finish them by yourself, so they sit in your freezer taking up space and you forget about them while they acquire freezer burn.

Over-processing

Over-processing waste is when you have processing steps that are not needed, and it is usually a result of poor tools or product design.

Examples:

- Your dishwasher is not working well, so you have to thoroughly scrub everything before it goes in.
- You make your grandmother's cake recipe and she insists that flour must be sifted first. One time you skip the sifting because you are in a hurry, and you notice no difference in the finished product.
- You typically make fruit smoothies with whatever fruit is in season, which you wash and then freeze before adding to your blender. After doing it this way for a while, you discover that frozen fruit from the store is comparable in price and the finished smoothies taste the same.

Transport

Transport waste is the movement of things from one place to another.

Examples:

- You clean the downstairs bathroom first, and then carry your cleaning supplies to the upstairs bathroom.
- You run up and down the stairs putting things away throughout the day.
- You are cleaning up the yard and keep running to the compost bin carrying armfuls of yard waste.
- You make a trip upstairs to get something because you forgot to bring it downstairs last time you were up there.

Waiting

Waiting is time wasted due to a holdup so you can't move on to the next step.

Examples:

- The dishwasher is full of dirty dishes already and you are just finishing dinner. What to do with the dishes piling up in the sink?
- It's potty training time for your toddler but every visit to the bathroom involves much waiting while your toddler sings and asks a million questions.

Motion

Motion of people is waste in the form of walking, searching, carrying, reaching, turning, etc. It is closely related to transport waste, but it focuses on the movement of people.

Examples:

- You make three trips to unload groceries from the car because you don't have hands to carry so many bags.

- When loading up the car, you run back and forth searching for keys and other things you need as you remember them.
- You are preparing dinner on a cluttered counter so your recipe and the stations of your prep work are spread all over the kitchen. You move around more than necessary.

Inventory

Inventory waste is stockpiling and not using an item before it is obsolete. Anything that takes up space but isn't needed right now is inventory. Inventory wastes both the resources used to acquire the excess goods, and also the real estate in your home where the goods are stored.

Examples:

- You buy produce and don't finish it before it goes bad.
- You buy clothes because you like them even though they don't fit your lifestyle or they don't match the other items in your closet.
- Your gift closet is brimming at the seams, but the gifts never seem to be a right fit for the people you are giving them to.

Now that you've got waste on your mind, I challenge you to start looking for it in your day to day life. Brainstorm a few examples of your own and jot them down below. Or, if you prefer, keep these types of waste in the back of your mind and as you encounter them in your tasks, flip back to this section and take note below.

Rework

____

____

____

Overproduction

____

____

____

Over-processing

____

____

____

Transport

____

____

____

Waiting

____

____

____

Motion

____

____

____

Inventory

____

____

____

Maybe you are thinking, "I don't really see why it's important to look for waste. It seems like that's a waste of my time. If something was wasteful I would have already stopped doing it." It's understandable why you might see it that way. However, think of it like this. If you put in a little extra effort to find *hidden* waste in the things you do all the time and you remove it, however small, it is an investment that will pay off in the long run because every time you do that task you will save yourself a little time, money, energy, etc. If you reduce waste from many tasks, and you reap those benefits over and over again each time that those tasks are repeated, those savings will pay off in your overall quality of life.

4

Organization

You are the engineer of your own home. You are the expert on what tasks add value to your family's life, what resources you have to work with, and the strengths and weaknesses of each person in your family. It is up to you to design a domestic plan that serves you and your loved ones well. There are five steps that

have proven to be effective for organizing your space and your life to be both functional and efficient. In *Lean Thinking*[3], these are called the "5S" principles: Sort, Systemize, Shine, Standardize,

---

[3] James P. Womack and Daniel T. Jones, *Lean Thinking: Banish Waste and Create Wealth in Your Corporation* (New York: Free Press, 2003).

and Sustain. The blueprint for implementing these tools is given below.

Start by sorting the things you actually use from the things you don't. Tackle one room at a time, and sort by item type. Your closet is a good place to start. Begin by gathering every shirt you own from your drawers, shelves, and hangers, and laying them out on your bed. Then pick each one up, one by one, and ask yourself, "Do I use this? Will I use it in the near future? Does this add value to my life?" If the answer is no, give yourself permission to remove that item from the space it takes in your home and in your life. When you have finished all your tops, move onto bottoms, accessories, etc.

You may be the type who likes to get this task over with in one fell swoop. It can be done this way! But some of us find it more manageable to break this up into fifteen-minute increments, or one type of item each day. Monday you might tackle shirts, Tuesday you sort through pants, Wednesday you purge accessories, etc.

With time you can sort like this through every area of your house until you've been through all your belongings, including toiletries, food, hobby supplies, books, kitchen items, and more. Remember that your life will be simpler with less stuff to manage, and you will be left with only the things you actually like and use.

If you are finding that this process is hard, imagine the end result of a decluttered home. What would it be like to not have to dig through your closet to find something you truly love to wear? How much would you enjoy having people over if you didn't have to shove everything in closets before you open the door? What creative hobbies would you use your basement for if it wasn't piled high with boxes and stuff you rarely use? Remember, if it's highly unlikely that you will need an item again and the item can easily be replaced, don't hesitate to get rid of it.

If you are hung up on all the money you've wasted on things you haven't used much or at all, decide now to be more particular about what you buy in the future. Don't let the guilt of past purchasing mistakes keep you from getting those things out of your life. You will not be able to recoup the costs of those items (not even close!) but you *can* recoup the space they have held hostage for so long.

Think of it this way. Every material possession you own takes up real estate in your home. If you enjoy math, you might even be able to figure out how much each square foot of space costs you in rent or mortgage payment. If you look at items in terms of the space they take up, is that item worth the real estate? This makes "large junk" look more like low-hanging fruit when it comes to purging unnecessary items. Your things aren't paying you rent, but some of them are unwelcome house guests that it's time to kick to the curb!

Systemize

Once you have purged through all the items in a category, the next step is to organize what's left in a way that makes sense. In general, you want to have everything visible when you are looking at what you have. For example, on a bookshelf you can see spines of every book and you might group books of a similar topic together. If you apply the same logic to your pantry, sides of boxes should be visible and baskets or bins can group like items for easy access. One way to make many small items visible is to hang a clear vinyl shoe organizer on the back of a door and sort miscellaneous (but still necessary/useful/loved) items in there so they are visible. This can work just as well in a pantry as in a gift closet, cleaning closet, or craft closet. The key here is whatever system you come up with for organizing the items you actually want to keep, be sure to put the items back in their designated homes after you use them. The reason for this is two-fold. First, if they are not where they belong then they are actually cluttering up your living space. Second, if they are not where they belong, then when you are looking for them you will have a harder time finding them and might even buy them again in a pinch.

For items that get used up, like toiletries, cleaning supplies, non-perishable and perishable food items, and office supplies, an inventory management system can help ensure you are neither running out nor stockpiling things unnecessarily. One way to do this is to create master lists of consumable goods in your home. This can be done with the use of apps on your phone, but if you prefer to work with a hard copy, read on.

You can start this by taking inventory of your pantry, bathroom drawers, medicine cabinet, and cleaning closet. Write down every item that you would replace when you run out. Group together like items on the list so you can easily find what you need. Place a check box to the left of each item. Type out and print off each list, and laminate it or put it into a protective sleeve. Then place each list in a place that makes sense to you. A pantry list can be taped to the wall inside the pantry. A fridge list can be placed on the top or side of the fridge. A bathroom list can

Fridge & Freezer Inventory

✓ Check when you need to buy

FRIDGE

- ○ Milk
- ○ Eggs
- ○ Yogurt- plain
- ○ Creamer
- ○ Butter
- ○ ___________________
- ○ ___________________
- ○ ___________________
- ○ ___________________

- ○ Apples
- ○ Oranges
- ○ Fruits- in season
- ○ Salad
- ○ Veggies- in season
- ○ ___________________
- ○ ___________________
- ○ ___________________
- ○ ___________________

- ○ Ketchup
- ○ Mustard
- ○ Mayo
- ○ Relish
- ○ Tomato Paste
- ○ Pickles
- ○ Minced garlic
- ○ Minced ginger
- ○ ___________________
- ○ ___________________
- ○ ___________________
- ○ ___________________

- ○ Ranch
- ○ Italian dressing
- ○ ___________________

- ○ ___________________
- ○ ___________________
- ○ ___________________

- ○ Parmesan
- ○ Shredded cheese
- ○ Sliced cheese
- ○ Turkey Lunchmeat
- ○ ___________________
- ○ ___________________
- ○ ___________________

FREEZER

- ○ Ice Cream
- ○ Bananas
- ○ Bread
- ○ Popsicles
- ○ Frozen Pizza
- ○ Flatbread
- ○ Quiche
- ○ Cilantro
- ○ Chicken Breasts
- ○ ___________________
- ○ ___________________
- ○ ___________________
- ○ ___________________
- ○ ___________________
- ○ ___________________
- ○ ___________________
- ○ ___________________
- ○ ___________________
- ○ ___________________
- ○ ___________________
- ○ ___________________

go on the backside of your bathroom cabinet under the sink. When you are about a week from running out of something, check it off on your list using a dry erase pen or washable crayon. Glance at your lists when you are going to the store where you usually purchase those items.

When you are creating this list, you may start to realize that you have quite a stash of expired vitamins, bottles of shampoos from brands you stopped using years ago, and many different kinds of laundry detergent. There are a few different reasons for the stockpiling. You may have seen an item at a good price and bought a huge supply. Or, you may have forgotten you had an item so you bought more. If the first is the reason, that habit might be broken if you begin to weigh the cost of the real estate that stockpile of goods will take in your home. If your 20 large bags of chips at $.99 each isn't worth the half a closet it takes to store it in for the next year it will take you to use them up, you probably shouldn't buy them. This might be an extreme example, but the principle applies on a smaller scale as well to things like moisturizer and toothpaste. If the stockpiling was due to forgetting what you had, the inventory management sheet should help you avoid wasteful duplicate purchases in the future. Avoid buying anything unless you are actually running low. One benefit of using the list for items you don't use often is that if you are running low on something like cough medicine, you can mark it on the list and wait until you see it on sale. If you knew you needed it, it would be worthwhile to purchase it before you needed it again if you were down to the last few doses.

Sanitize

Once you have sorted and systemized your belongings, the next step is to sanitize. This is the part where you dust, sweep, scrub, and shine every nook and cranny of your living and storage space. This

should be a whole lot less daunting if you have already purged many things from your home and implemented a system for keeping your remaining things organized. It doesn't have to be done all at once, but it should all be done at some point. Aside from the health benefits that come with having a clean house, this will also allow you to see areas that need attention. It becomes easier to spot a leak under the sink when you have sorted through the piles of plastic bags stashed down there. The odorous sticky spot on your pantry floor from a bag of potatoes that rotted a few months back can finally be scrubbed off now that you can actually see the pantry floor. A home management routine guru, Marla Cilley (aka. "Fly Lady"), says in her book *Sink Reflections* that every room has a "shiny sink".[4] What she means is that no matter how bad of a state your home is in, if you tackle the project of cleaning one key focal point in the room, and then diligently work to maintain its "shiny" status, the other areas of that room will follow suit. You will begin to take pride in that sink, or table, or floor, and it will motivate you to not only keep that clean but to take care of other areas in the room. Skeptical? Try it! See if deep cleaning and maintaining one targeted area spurs you on to bigger and better cleaning efforts.

Standardize

After the initial deep cleaning, creating standardized processes for cleaning, maintenance, and other tasks that add value to your home life is the next natural step. You can find tools to help you with this task on my blog at www.more-than-rubies.com/LifestyleRedesigned.

---

[4] Marla Cilley, *Sink Reflections* (New York: Bantam Books, 2004).

Start by listing the tasks that should be *non-negotiable* for you every day. For me, I would like to see that I never miss a day of reading my Bible, working out, reading to my little ones, getting dinner on the table, cleaning the kitchen, etc. Those items would go on my "Daily Tasks" list.

Daily Tasks:

-
-
-
-
-
-
-
-

Next, list what items you would ideally like to accomplish at least once a week (ex: laundry, menu planning, shop, clean bathrooms, vacuum, mop, dust).

Weekly Tasks:

-
-
-
-
-

-
-
-

-
-
-

Continue on with monthly and quarterly tasks, such as: pay bills, get oil changed, clean baseboards, clean fridge, purge clutter, file mail, clean the car, file receipts. Remember to think in terms of value to your family. Don't create your list based on what you think you're capable of. Even if it seems like more than you were ever able to do before don't leave anything out of the brainstorming. You'd be surprised how much more efficiently you work when you don't have to think about what to work on next.

Monthly and Quarterly Tasks:

-
-
-
-
-
-
-

-
-
-
-
-
-
-

Hopefully by now you are starting to get excited about what you can accomplish with a good system in place.

Now it's time to decide when during your day, week, month, or quarter you want to accomplish these duties and populate your time management system. If you are using a calendar app, it is so simple to set up a task to repeat at a regular interval, and even easier to move it if your schedule changes. You can also use to-do lists for daily tasks instead of laying out your schedule minute-by-minute. This is my favorite way to keep track of the

Routine Tasks

Every Day	Weekly	
Morning	Monday	Tuesday
Afternoon	Wednesday	Thursday
Evening	Friday	Saturday & Sunday

more frequent tasks, and save the calendar events for monthly and non-regular items. Above is a template available on more-than-rubies.com/LifestyleRedesigned to help you create a system.

Managing the information in your schedule and creating to-do-lists makes up the bulk of getting organized, so if you've already made it this far, the hardest part of time management is behind you!

Now you have a bird's eye view of what you are working towards during the day, week, month, etc. Part of standardizing your work, however, is deciding what your best practices are for each task and process. This is where you, the CEO in Your Home, Inc., set the standards. You decide how each of those tasks needs to be accomplished. You decide where everything should go. You are your own domestic engineer, so design the life that you value most. Only you know what makes you happy. Once you have outlined how your day-to-day life should look, it is up to you and your family to maintain the standards you set. Having it on paper, whether in the form of charts, to-do-lists, or calendars, creates a form of accountability. When you face decisions throughout the day about how to use your time, you have a clear visual outline of what is important to you and when you should tackle each task. Without it, you are subject to doing only what you feel like doing at any given moment instead of what you truly value in the big picture.

There is a huge sense of accomplishment that comes with having a plan and sticking to it. Do you get a thrill of excitement when you cross something off your list? I know I do! Let that work to your advantage. My favorite way to keep track of tasks is to stick my regular task list, broken up by daily, weekly, and monthly items, into a plastic sheet protector and mark things off with a dry erase pen as I complete them. At the end of each day, week, and month I erase the respective sections and start over.

At this point you probably have a plan that you feel pretty good about. You might have even implemented those tasks lists by now. However, it will all be for naught if you don't find a way to maintain the awesome progress you've made. This is where habits come into play.

Habits

Once you have designed the life you value, the goal is to make most of your daily tasks into habits. Why? Because some things that add value to your life may not be things you really love doing. If you really don't enjoy it, then even if you remove waste from the process and learn how to do it well, it still might require effort to do. And if you have a few items like this that you've designed into every day, it can make keeping up with your plan feel burdensome. It will take discipline to do those things you just don't really want to do.

But the good news is that once you make those things habits, then they won't require discipline to do. You won't have to use willpower to accomplish those things once they become habits. Don't believe me? How about the example of brushing your teeth. If you are like most people, you probably do this task twice a day without much effort. You probably don't stand at the sink each morning and evening and ask yourself, "Am I going to brush them this time?" It's not a conscious decision you have to make because it's a habit. It doesn't require your reserve of willpower or self-discipline to do it. This is a truth we can apply and work for our benefit in other tasks.

You see, willpower is like a muscle. When we have to use our willpower a lot throughout the day we eventually get tired of making good decisions. It becomes more challenging to do the things we have already decided on paper that we intend to do. Other factors like sleep can also influence our willpower capacity. You can read more about this in the book, *Willpower: Rediscovering the Greatest Human Strength.* This is where establishing habits is the key to our success. Every one of those tasks that we turn into a habit becomes one that doesn't require us to make a conscious decision of our will to complete. Let me say it in a different way. If you can turn it into a habit, it will no longer require your willpower "muscle" to do it.[5] Isn't that good news?

Root Cause Analysis

In addition to making tasks into habits, we have to create a culture of addressing problems and deviations immediately. When you see something not happening as it should, do a root cause analysis to figure out the underlying cause. The easiest way to do this is to ask, "Why did this happen"? Then ask "why" again, and again, and again, as many times as it takes until you get down to the root of the problem. Let's look at an example.

The trash can is overflowing.

Why?

Because it didn't go out on garbage day.

Why?

Because Dylan didn't have time to do it before school.

Why?

Because he didn't get up when the alarm clock went off.

Why?

---

[5] Roy F. Baumeister and John Tierney, *Willpower: Rediscovering the Greatest Human Strength* (New York, NY: Penguin Books, 2012).

Because he isn't a morning person and wants to get as much sleep as he can before school.

The root cause is that the person responsible for taking out the garbage has a hard time getting up in the morning and didn't allow time for this task. Because we have identified it, we can do something about this problem to keep it from happening again. What if Dylan makes it a habit to take out the trash and put the cans out the night before, since he is a night owl anyway? This makes better use of his strengths. He can try doing it that way to see if it fixes the problem. If not, or if new problems arise, he can keep adjusting the plan until he gets it right.

Maintenance

When it comes to the stuff in our house, maintaining a clutter-free environment might be challenging if you don't change how you view the stuff. When shopping, remember the real estate concept mentioned earlier in this chapter. Before buying something, ask yourself three questions: "Is it necessary?

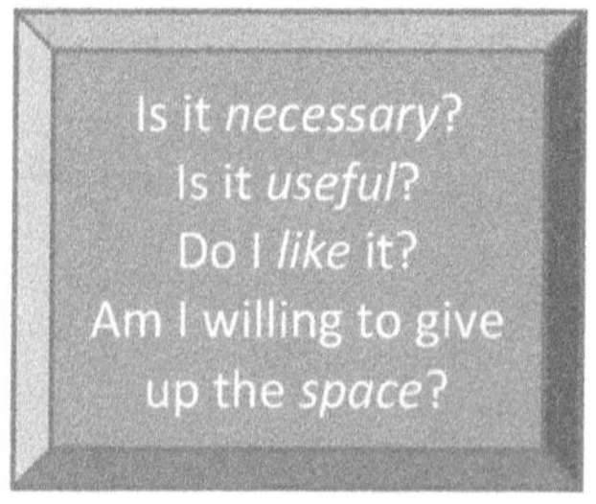

Is it useful? Do I like it?" If it passes those criteria, then also ask yourself, "Am I willing to give up the space this will require?" Or, "Is it worth the real estate in my home?" If you think about things in this way *before* you buy them you can avoid the trouble of filling up your home with unnecessary stuff. Periodic purging might still be necessary but you don't have to let your house fill up with clutter again. It is much easier to maintain than to let things get out of hand and then have to do something drastic to regain your ground.

This might go without saying but if you design a lifestyle you value, you will need to revisit your plan regularly to see if you are actually following it. If not, do a root cause analysis to see why you or your family members aren't following through, and see if it's the plan that needs amending or if the issue could be fixed with more training, tweaking the process, or another simple adjustment.

It will initially take discipline and repetition to establish those good habits. Don't get the idea that if it's not easy then it isn't going to work for your lifestyle. If you have decided that it's valuable to you, then commit to finding a way to make it work. When it finally clicks and becomes a habit that serves you and your family well, you will see that it was worth the effort.

5

If you're like me, you've marveled at some amazing storage and organization solutions before. They probably caught your eye because they were nice to look at and made it easy to find what you need. Our eyes and brains appreciate being able to see things clearly labeled or visible in plain sight when we need them. But visual cues can do so much more for us.

In addition to helping you stay organized, visual cues can help you notice and track problems, signal when an action needs to be taken, list steps to keep you on track, and keep important information easily accessible. Ready to see what I mean?

Visible Storage

Let's start with visible storage for quickly locating and returning items. Your eyes are your greatest tool in creating a storage system that allows you to find the correct locations of things easily and accurately. One strategy you can learn from a bookshelf is that storing items in an upright profile view allows you to get a preview of all or most of the items, with minimal visual space, and minimal disruption to remove or replace an item. This same strategy can be applied to clothes, a pantry, a linen closet, and a host of other items.

In her book, *The Life Changing Magic of Tidying Up*[6], Marie Kondo teaches how to organize your clothes in this way. She advocates storing most clothing in drawers, grouped by type, and folded in such a way that each item can be visible from a profile view. For example, shirts are folded into a rectangular shape so that when they are stood on end, they create a sort of filing system in which one folded crease of each item is visible from the top of the open drawer. This makes it easy to find what you are looking for instead of always picking what's on top out of convenience, or digging to the bottom and having to pull the whole pile out. It becomes easy to see when you are running out of something, and also simplifies the task of putting things back in the right place because you can slip the shirt back in between as you would do with a folder in a filing cabinet. Apply this same logic to things that are stored in boxes in a pantry or elsewhere, with the

------

[6] Marie Kondo and Cathy Hirano, *The Life-Changing Magic of Tidying Up* (London: Vermilion, 2014).

thinnest side standing vertically like a spine. Digging will be a thing of the past.

Another visible storage concept is color coding. This is especially helpful for identifying similar looking things by type or by owner. For example, if your household has a plethora of prescription medications in a basket, you can place a colored dot on the lid corresponding to the person who uses each one. When you are glancing at all the lids, you can quickly find the correct bottle. In our home we also color code drinking glasses using silicone bracelets that we have acquired from various events. Color coding minimizes errors when you are tired or distracted.

Another visual cue for storing oddly shaped items is to mark their spot on the ground or in the drawer. You might create a parking lot for kid cars, trikes, and bikes with masking tape on your covered porch outside. Or you might trace tools onto a drawer liner or pegboard to ensure they go back to the right place after use. If there is one spot for each item, it is also easy to glance and see what is missing.

If there are instructions or recipes you'd like to have quick access to, labeled tabs are another easy tool your eyes can use to find what you're looking for. If a cookbook or manual is one you refer to often, don't feel bad about marking it up with permanent tabs, highlighters, notes, etc. These things will only make it more functional and more personal.

Labeling

Ideally it would be easiest if we could see all the items of one type in one glance. However, when items are small or oddly shaped (like toys, shoes, or pantry snacks) it often makes sense to keep them in a bin or basket. Labels on the outside can help ensure these things are easy to find and are put in the right place. If your goal is to get kids to put away their own toys and shoes, but they aren't confident readers yet, you may need a graphical labeling system. Always keep your audience in mind. You can make cleanup responsibilities easier and also help visitors stick to your system by using appropriate labels.

Calendars are an indispensable tool in the home, but as the number of family members, activities, and responsibilities grows, the information shown on them becomes more complex. A different colored pen or highlighter assigned to each person can simplify what you are looking at—your brain can tune into one color over one time period, or focus on all the activities on one day. If it makes more sense to differentiate calendar entries by type or importance, this can be done using colors as well whether on a calendar app or a paper calendar. Certain irregular tasks from your to-do-list may be integrated into your calendar using sticky notes so they can be removed after completion.

Keep Important Information Accessible

Another form of labeling is making the important information stand out. For perishable groceries, writing the expiration date on the item in bold numbers with a marker can help you to use those things before they go bad. On prescription bottles, you can re-copy the dosage information onto the lid or another blank spot using a bold marker (ex: 3x/day with food) to avoid mistakes and confusion. You can also write the start date and time on a bottle of antibiotics. Always double check that you've labeled it correctly when working with medicine.

If you have a recipe or instructions that you use frequently but you haven't committed to memory yet, try attaching it to the primary ingredient. For example, tape a laminated copy of your bread recipe to the bag of flour. If you have a complicated laundry routine for your cloth diapers, display a quick summary of the instructions on your washer or the detergent container. Perhaps you are a tea connoisseur and you like to follow the precise brewing time for each variety. Write it in bold letters inside the lid of the box or on a note inside the cabinet door so you don't have to go hunting for it every time.

Here are a few more examples of keeping the important information handy:

- An inventory list on the pantry door
- A packing checklist in a plastic sleeve for reuse
- A bucket list displayed proudly on the refrigerator
- Neon sticky notes strategically placed around the house for your house sitter
- A white board keeping track of your weekend task list
- A menu planning display

What others can you think of?

____

____

Actionable Cues

Visual cues can signal when it's time to perform an action. Are there certain tasks that you find it difficult to remember to do in a timely manner? Maybe you rationalize putting it off because there is no clear indicator that it has to be done immediately. Do you wait to do laundry until the hamper is overflowing but then it won't all fit in one load anyway? You might end up with one and a half loads of dark clothes to wash. A line of tape inside your pre-sorted hamper at the level of a full load can signal to you to start a load when it's filled to that line.

Or, you can replace your hamper with one that is just the right size for a full load, and when it's full you know to start a load.

Similarly, you can draw a line on your milk jug, laundry detergent, contact solution, or other containers to signal to you to add the item to your shopping list when the contents fall below the indicator line. Or, if you have a stockpile of something you use frequently, like cans of soda or individual yogurts cups, you can put a note on one near the back of your stockpile. This method only works if you actually follow through on the next step when you see the indicator and train others to do the same. However, it can be a useful tool to keep you from running out of something important.

Performance Tracking

A visual system can be highly effective for noticing and tracking performance and problems. A visual log can provide a rewarding (or telling) display for tracking goals, whether related to health, fitness, academics, or personal achievements. If you have a consistency goal, track it with a small sticker added to your calendar or planner for each day you performed that task. This can help you to notice patterns that may be related to other factors. For example, you may notice that you rarely ever made it out for your daily run when you watched your favorite TV show the night before. Or, you can feel the satisfaction of a job well done when you see a week or month of consistency and reward yourself with predetermined prizes. For goals measured quantitatively in other ways, you can create a simple drawing to color in different portions as you reach milestones. It's encouraging to be able to see your progress visually.

Kids' chores can be displayed and tracked for a reward system using visual graphics. A graphic for each task can remind them of what they need to do, even if they aren't reading yet. Completed tasks can be marked with a dry erase pen or stickers. Alternately, having the graphics on markers that can be moved

 Sam	Responsibilities	Jenny 
Make your bed		Make your bed
Get dressed		Get dressed
Put on shoes and socks		Put on shoes and socks
Brush teeth		Brush teeth
Potty before naps and bedtime		Pee on potty when awake
Finish your meals		Finish your meals
Take plate to sink		Take plate to sink
Clean up spills	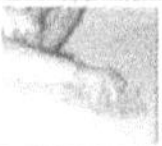	Clean up spills
Put away toys		Put away toys
Practice piano x 10 songs		Practice Blackbirds x2
Please and Thank You		Asking nicely without screaming
Obey the 1st time		Obey the 1st time

from "to-do" to "in-progress" to "done!" can make the process especially fun. Make the system age appropriate and understandable to its users.

Another example for tracking achievements is to physically move something from one pile to another when it is completed. If you have a goal of reading 15 particular books in the next year, designate a shelf for keeping track of them. You can create a large, fun divider to place between the ones you've read and the ones you haven't. You can also move the completed ones to another shelf entirely and relish in watching it fill up. If the item or task is too big to be moved, a marker like a clothespin, popsicle stick, or a sticky note can represent the task. If you get great satisfaction from crossing things off a to-do list, you should try the physical act of moving a task from one pile to another!

Visual cues can be used to monitor any aspect of a task. You may have some extensive projects or goals you are working on. For example, if you are hosting a Christmas party you will have many different pieces to plan. Many of the tasks will happen simultaneously and some will be dependent on others being completed. Outline the tasks in great detail, and then use indicators, like a colored dot or sticky flag next to the task, to show you when it's in progress or complete. Colors can indicate which to start next and allow you to delegate tasks to others because you have a comprehensive picture of what needs to happen.

Are you seeing what I'm seeing now? There are so many ways we can benefit from using visual tools. Organize things with visibility as the goal. Label what can't be seen in a way that the user can understand. Keep important information within sight or easily accessible. Log progress toward goals, and use indicators to show the status of projects. All of these visual cues help to increase the efficiency and accuracy of tasks and simplify our lives and the lives of others.

6

Gaining Skills

Do you ever find yourself wishing you had a cleaning lady, a personal chef, a gardener, a secretary, a workout coach, a nanny, a handyman, a professional organizer, or a seamstress at your fingertips? There may be some tasks that you simply hate for no reason at all. However, there might be some tasks you wish you could delegate because you just aren't confident in your ability to do them, or you feel you just aren't naturally gifted in that area. To some extent that may be true, but it doesn't have to be the end of the story. With the right mindset you can learn to conquer some of those tough tasks.

Your Mindset

If you have already made up your mind that you aren't naturally good at something and you believe you can't do anything about it, then you won't.[7] You will be limited by your own mindset. If that feels true to you about certain things, you need to hear this. Repeat after me: "I can learn hard things."

A fixed mindset says "I am not good at this and I won't ever be." With that outlook, you believe that you are helpless to change the situation so you resign to just not dwell on it and move on to the next thing.

A growth mindset says, "I can learn most anything if I put in the effort." With that outlook you can take practical steps to change the situation. Because, in reality, if some of your dislike for certain tasks stems from your inability to do them well, then gaining skills can only help the situation. You can learn more about the growth mindset from Stanford psychology professor Carol S. Dweck, Ph.D., in *Mindset: The New Psychology of Success*.

Learn Hard Things

Maybe you are overwhelmed by your children, and you find yourself doing a lot more yelling than you would like. While some things are learned by experience, you can jump ahead of the power curve by listening to parenting podcasts, reading a book on something you haven't figured out yet, or even attending a community group like MOPS (Mothers of Preschoolers) where you can learn from other parents through their experiences.

If picking up after yourself (or your children) is your downfall, maybe an audiobook on decluttering and daily tidying will help you free your family from some of the things that are causing you the biggest headaches. You are not doomed to stay stuck in a clutter jungle forever. Learn a new skill and a new way of looking

---

[7] Carol S. Dweck, *Mindset: the New Psychology of Success* (New York: Ballantine Books, 2016).

at things, and then put it into practice immediately to see if it makes your life easier.

Meal planning is another prime example. If nobody has ever sat down and taught you that it is helpful to plan your meals ahead of time, you might regularly find yourself staring at the fridge at 5 o'clock wondering what to make. There are many strategies and tools for planning meals out there, including online programs with recipes and shopping lists. Or, a simple weekly meal planning board with index card tags naming your favorite recipes to clip in for each day could suffice. The key is that you intentionally make meal planning a discipline, however you choose to do it. And if you don't know how to do it, then learn how. Ask others how they do it and what tools they use. Keep an eye out for ideas when you are in someone's house. Utilize Pinterest for ideas for planning, not just for gathering recipes.

I grew up in a family in which my dad worked as a professional chef in a five-star restaurant. He knew every food prep trick in the book, and yet he never taught me those skills. As an adult who lacked training, I found that cutting vegetables and meat were tedious tasks. However, I would sometimes watch cooking shows because I was fascinated by the science and art behind cooking. I would watch the way the chefs rock the knife to cut veggies quickly and try to mimic what the professionals did. I would watch baking shows and absorb all I could. I also started to watch my grandmother and my mother-in-law cook their specialties, while I would ask questions and write down their recipes. I would take online classes on Craftsy.com to learn to prepare very specific types of foods that I couldn't learn elsewhere.

In the information age that we live in, we have access to so infinitely more information than our parents did. Blogs, YouTube videos, articles, and online classes are just a few clicks away. We also have access to books from the library, and even audiobooks for those who can't find time to sit down and read a book. We have interest groups, meetups, and conferences on every subject you could imagine. If you desire to learn something, you can find a way to learn it.

Learn from Those You Know

We also have our peers and elders to reach out to. Do you have a friend that bakes amazing sourdough bread, and you'd like to know how to do that yourself? Instead of meeting up for coffee next time, ask your friend to come over to teach you some bread-making basics. Ask for a list of supplies and ingredients beforehand, so you will feel confident that you can achieve the same results on your home turf by yourself next time. Same thing goes for skills like budgeting, gardening, working out, etc. Most people are flattered to be asked to help when you recognize and appreciate the skillset they have. And, the bonus is that you get to spend quality time with the person in a very intentional way.

Shift Your Perspective

It is time to retrain your mind. When you admire a gift or skill someone has that would be really helpful in your life, or maybe even feel a twinge of jealousy when you see it in action, shift your perspective. Instead of believing that skill is for them only and you will never be good at it, condition yourself to say, "Can you teach me a little about that?" Having a teachable attitude will allow you to glean some of their wisdom and can help you get past a place where you have previously been stuck.

When there is a particular skill set that will take some time to develop, seek out a mentor. For example, rather than saying, "Can you help me learn how to make your amazing lasagna?", a better approach might be to ask, "Would you be willing to meet with me a few times and walk me through how you plan and cook meals for your family?". Mentorship is an ongoing relationship that is intentional about sharing a skill (or many). To get the most out of a mentoring relationship, we must be humble enough to share openly about where we are at and be willing to receive critical feedback along with the encouragement.

Here are a few life skills you might want to consider for focused training:

- cooking,
- meal planning,
- nutrition,
- basic home repairs,
- changing your oil,
- lawn care,
- balancing your budget,
- app tools on your phone,
- workouts to keep you healthy and give you energy,
- child development,
- couponing,
- woodworking, and
- basic sewing.

What are some skills you could work on improving so you can be more effective and satisfied with the tasks you do most often?

____

____

What are some practical steps you can take to gain skills in those areas?

____

____

____

We all have blind spots. You may not even realize you aren't good at something or that you lack skills in an area. Sometimes you don't know what you are missing. This is an opportunity to ask those closest to you to share where they think your skills need improvement. If you are truly in a position of wanting to grow, don't let their remarks offend you. Let them be like a mirror to help you see where your weak spots are.

Speaking of those close to you, if you have a spouse or kids, you will work more cohesively as a team if you take the time to offer them training as well. You can lighten your load if you can delegate tasks to others who are clear on the directions and have learned the necessary skills to do it. Make learning tasks fun!

For example, if you teach your two-year-old to help you empty the dryer then she can do that task for you while you are putting the next load into the washer. Also, training kids to pick up their toys and labeling the bins or shelves with pictures of what goes there can save you some work and also keep them occupied while you do something else. You may need to hold their attention with clean up music like the Dora the Explorer "Clean-Up Song." Make it a game so they enjoy it! Kids can be taught to pack their own lunch and snacks, match socks from the laundry, and so much more. Do a web search for "age-appropriate chores" and you'll see some more great ideas. The first few times you may have to help or gently correct their work, but eventually they will gain confidence in their abilities and these chores will become habits that they do well. Praise them for the little successes, with the end goal in mind.

When it comes to your spouse, you can each learn from one another's strengths. If you teach your spouse how to chop veggies, make the breakfast smoothies for the whole family, change the oil in the car, or how to program the sprinklers, then when you are tied up with other tasks those things don't have to wait for you. If they have the mindset that certain chores are theirs and others are yours because that's what you each are good at, share with them about the growth mindset. Take the time to learn one another's tasks. It will help you each to do your parts better when you understand how your roles intertwine, but also allow you each to cross over and share one another's loads when your partner is swamped.

Whether with a spouse or a child, if you take a little time to train them in lean principles and work with them in developing processes that work well for everyone, that little investment can lead to big payoff in the long term. Communication and openness are essential here. You and your spouse (or children, or roommate) can look at a process together and talk about what works and what doesn't work. Where each of you are seeing waste on your own end, another brain working on it can help bring creative ideas to the table to solve long-standing problems. That second perspective can be invaluable in creating order in your home and encourage buy-in.

7

Flow and the Experience of Work

It is so easy to let your home be filled with projects and tasks that are currently in progress. Laundry gazes at you longingly from the basket as you pass by, and wonders when you will fold it and return it to its home. Dishes hold awkward poses in the sink waiting to get a rinse under the faucet and to then be proudly stood up in the dishwasher. Dust bunnies mock you from under the coffee table, thinking today will surely not be the day you actually decide to vacuum the downstairs. And those club-sized packages of paper goods you purchased without a clear vision of where you would store them form a modern-art sort of brick wall in the entryway. All these tasks have been stalled like a car that ran out of gas, and their mid-process existence in your life lends a sort of chaos as you always seem to be behind. You had good intentions when you began each one, but for various reasons, you stopped mid-task and jumped to another.

Let's switch to manufacturing mode for a moment here. One of the most remarkable outcomes that lean companies experience is a dramatically reduced turnaround time from when an order is placed to the time it is delivered to the customer.[8] The peripheral benefits of having a faster turnaround time are that less has to be done ahead of time, less things have to take up space in the factory while they wait for the next step, and there is less space needed for storage at the same rate of production.

Take a walk around the company that is Your Home, Inc., and notice all the projects and tasks in progress. Note them here:

____

____

____

____

____

____

____

____

____

____

Not only do they take up physical space, but they also take up space in your brain and in your schedule. If you only had one or two going on at any given moment, wouldn't you feel like you

---

[8] James P. Womack and Daniel T. Jones, *Lean Thinking: Banish Waste and Create Wealth in Your Corporation* (Riverside: Free Press, 2010).

have a bit more freedom to relax? Let's look at how you can improve flow and reduce waiting so you can make that happen.

The first step is to draw a diagram of how materials and information flow in a process. The following example will track the Johnson Family's dishes through a typical cycle of use.

As you can see, this process is a repeating cycle, like many others in the Johnson home. The dishes begin in the cabinet. Little Jenny Johnson carries the dishes from the cabinet to the table and sets it for dinner. The Johnsons eat dinner together and then each person scrapes food scraps into the garbage and carries their dishes to the sink. Sometimes the sink is full of pots and pans, so the dishes are placed on the counter. While the kids are doing homework, Mr. Johnson rinses the dishes and loads them in the dishwasher. The pots and pans get hand-washed and placed in the drying rack next to the sink. Mr. Johnson runs the dishwasher. In the morning, Mrs. Johnson opens the dishwasher. She removes the dry dishes and puts them away. She puts away the pots and pans which are now dry from the night before. She then shakes out the containers that still have drips on them and lets them dry in the rack next to the sink. Later in the morning, Mrs. Johnson puts away the containers. Throughout the morning and afternoon each family member places their dishes in the sink or on the counter after meals.

If you were a fly on the wall in the Johnson kitchen, there are two dish scenarios you might observe, depending on the time of day. Most times of the day you would see some dishes in the sink and maybe a few on the counter. If you flew in after dinner time, you might not see any dishes because they would all be in a running dishwasher, except the pots and pans drying. If you happened to land in the morning, you'd see some containers in the drying rack and a few dirty dishes piling up in the sink.

Throughout this example, you may have noticed that the dishes were the thing we followed through the process. This is important to mapping the process. You might be tempted to hone in on the dishwasher and note what happens there at various points in the daily dish cycle. However, in order to spot waste in the process so you can remove it, you must focus on how the goods (or information) is moving through the process. In lean terms this is called "mapping the value stream".[9]

____

[9] James P. Womack and Daniel T. Jones, *Lean Thinking: Banish Waste and Create Wealth in Your Corporation* (New York: Free Press, 2003).

In the Johnson's dish process there are several areas of waste that show up when we map it out like this. First, there is Waiting. This comes in the form of the dishes that are piling up in and around the sink, and also the pots and pans and containers that dry in the dishrack. Waiting also occurs inside the dishwasher before it is run, and before it is emptied, but those aren't really an inconvenience to the Johnson Family because they are out of sight. Instead of the dishes waiting in limbo by the sink, what if each person, as they cleared their plate, brought it to the sink, rinsed it off and then placed it directly in the dishwasher? Of course, this would not work if the dishwasher was still full of clean dishes after a cycle, so Mrs. Johnson would have to empty it before breakfast.

The containers being placed in the drying rack in the morning are an example of rework and waiting that might be avoidable. They are washed and dried in the dishwasher, but water pools up in the small spaces and they don't fully dry. Mrs. Johnson shakes them out in the morning and puts them in the other rack to finish drying. However, if Mr. Johnson runs the dishwasher around 7pm and it finishes the drying cycle before he goes to bed that night, he can open it while the dishes are still fairly warm, shake out the containers that are still wet, and place them back in the dishwasher to finish drying while the dishwasher cools down. This moves the waiting to the overnight hours, saving a step in the morning. Then in the morning everything could be emptied straight to the cabinets. Or, if they live in a dry climate, could they just shake the containers out and put them away slightly damp without the lids on?

Do you see any other areas of waste? Dishes are put away in the cabinet and then brought to the table to be set. This could be both Motion and Transport waste. If the Johnson Family uses a formal dining table only for eating and not for other projects, it might be possible to set the table right from the dishwasher so it's always ready for dinner. This would be especially doable if the family typically eats breakfast at the kitchen counter. Can you think of any others examples of waste in this process?

Flow

When the goods or information of the value stream move from step to step with minimal waiting, we refer to this phenomenon as "flow."

Take dinner prep, for example. Here are the steps involved:

- Look at recipe.
- Pull out ingredients.
- Take out pans and utensils.
- Measure ingredients.
- Put away ingredients.
- Chop and prep fresh ingredients.
- Begin cooking.
- Wait for food to cook.
- Add ingredients.
- Wait for food to cook.
- Season to taste.
- Serve.
- Eat.
- Clean up pots and pans.

If you did each of those tasks in the order listed you might find cooking to be a long, tedious, and tiresome process even though it looks perfectly logical to do it that way. Let's look at the time it takes to do each of those tasks and see if we can improve the flow.

- Look at recipe (2 min).
- Pull out ingredients (2 min).
- Take out pans and utensils (1 min).
- Measure ingredients (3 min).
- Put away ingredients (2 min).
- Chop and prep fresh ingredients (20 min).
- Begin cooking (3 min).
- Wait for food to cook (10 min).
- Add ingredients (1 min).
- Wait for food to cook (15 min).
- Season to taste (1 min).
- Serve (1 min).
- Eat (time not counted).
- Clean up pots and pans (15 min).

There are two points in this process where waiting is necessary for the food to cook. However, if you can reorder the process so that the waiting time is filled with other necessary tasks, then it will no longer be waiting. What if you prep and measure only those ingredients you need right away and then start the cooking before prepping the rest? The ten minutes of wait time while onions are browning or water is coming to a boil seems to vanish as chopping and prepping fills that time. Then you have another chunk of cooking downtime after adding some ingredients. You decide to put away your ingredients and start cleaning up bowls, pans, and measuring utensils you are finished with in a race against your cooking timer. You've gotten most of the cleanup under way so you don't have to do it after eating. Cooking becomes less arduous when you remove some of the wait time.

Let's see how we did with flow.

- Look at recipe (2 min)

- Pull out ingredients (2 min)
- Take out pans and utensils (1 min)
- Measure ingredients (3 min)
- Chop and prep ingredients (10 min)
- Begin cooking (3 min)
- Wait for recipe to cook (10 min) + Continue to chop and prep (10 min)
- Add ingredients (1 min)
- Wait for recipe to cook (15 min) + Put away ingredients (2 min) + Clean up measuring cups, mixing bowls, some pans (10 min)
- Season to taste (1 min)
- Serve (1 min)
- Eat (time not counted)
- Finish cleaning pots and pans (5 min)

In all you have saved yourself about 22 minutes from the total time of 76 minutes. You reduced the time of making this meal by almost 1/3 from start to finish. That's pretty impressive!

You might be thinking that is not at all realistic. When you add in kids, phone calls, and other interruptions to the process it's not always so easy to use your time so strategically. To some degree that is true. However, each of us has some common, recurring interruptions that we can anticipate. For example, I know that one or both of my kids will wake up from their nap while I am preparing dinner, and will likely want some attention. I can plan to start my prep-work earlier in the day so that the meal can be already in the oven by the time they wake up. If that's not possible, I can have a snack and an activity ready for them so they can be occupied while I finish up. It's also important to remember that most kids don't need your undivided attention all of the time, but they do need it some of the time. If you know you will need to keep them occupied later in the day for a scheduled task, plan some quality one-on-one time earlier in the day so their emotional tanks will be filled up. If they aren't starved for attention you might be able to give them over to an exciting toy, book, or activity for a bit when you really need the time to focus.

What other common interruptions do you face that throw you off of your game? Do emails and texts pinging on your phone pull you away for ten minutes because you can't just glance at the preview? Perhaps putting the phone in another room and leaving it there unless it's actually ringing can keep you off the rabbit trail of distraction until you've completed a task. You don't have to succumb to everything that begs for your attention.

For both the predictable and unpredictable interruptions, the key is to address them quickly and get back to the task at hand, unless you consciously decide to switch to something else. Be mindful and intentional about your goals, both big and small. If the same distractions keep coming up, use the tools available to you to minimize them when possible. Do a root cause analysis by asking "Why did this happen?" until you get to the bottom of the issue. Come up with solutions and try them until they work. And when they stop working, try out new solutions.

If kids are the biggest challenge to your productivity, there are a few ways of handling it. If your attention is pulled away at a natural break in the task you are working on, you can wrap up what you are doing and resume the task later. If you are not near a stopping point, can you get the kids involved in what you are working on and use it as a teachable moment? Kids can be given age appropriate chores that, at a minimum, can keep them occupied while you work on a related task, or they can even help lighten your load. Make it fun for them. Young kids are often excited to be a part of what we are doing, and they feel a sense of pride when you acknowledge their helpfulness. Make a big deal of their task and let them feel the thrill of a job well done. They will be more apt to help out next time, and you might actually have a lighter load when they learn to do the task with excellence.

Why is it so important to find ways to remediate distractions? In this chapter you have seen how the value stream can flow when wait time is reduced, allowing tasks to be completed faster and leaving less ongoing projects in your home at one time. You may not have thought about how this might affect you personally.

Satisfaction in Work

Can you think of a hobby that, when you start doing it, you often get so immersed in it that you lose track of time? Hours can go by, and you are so deeply enjoying what you were doing that you forget about most everything else. What if I told you that you could feel that same feeling, to some degree, when you do other tasks too? In other words, it's not so much what you are actually doing at that moment that makes you feel so good that you lose track of time. It's actually the mental state that you get into. You are in the zone. This is sometimes referred to as "the flow", but to avoid confusion with process flow we will be using the term "the zone".

When you are in the zone, you are fully immersed in the task. You enjoy what you are doing. You are focused and energized. You could keep doing it a long time.

To get in the zone, you need a clear objective, a need for intense concentration, lack of interruptions and distractions, feedback on progress, and a sense of challenge.[10]

By working on a process in which the tasks flow, you are setting yourself up to work in the zone.

Wait as Intentional Rest

When you find yourself with wait times that you can't seem to fill with value-adding tasks, sometimes the next best thing is to intentionally rest during that time. We have conditioned ourselves to fill those times with social media, TV, and other things we find relaxing. However, sometimes those things cause the time to disappear down a black hole without leaving us truly feeling rested. The break extends indefinitely and then we look back at our time and wonder where it went. When rest is the most valuable thing you can do with your break, be intentional about it. Use that break for an activity that relaxes you, nourishes you, or fills your tank. Set a timer if necessary, and allow yourself to be fully present as you rest on purpose.

Challenge yourself to fill the wait times with things that add value, whether from the task in progress or others nearby. When that's not possible, use that time to rest, recoup, and refocus. Maybe the most valuable thing you can do while the laundry is drying is take your kids to play in the back yard. Play well and be fully present. You are filling their tanks with quality time and taking care of some of your most important customers. That is surely adding value to their lives.

---

[10] James P. Womack and Daniel T. Jones, *Lean Thinking: Banish Waste and Create Wealth in Your Corporation* (New York: Free Press, 2003), 64-65.

8

Using the Tools

By this point you have encountered a tool belt full of strategies for engineering your home life to have less waste and leave you more satisfied. You've defined the things that add value to your life, learned how to identify the 7 types of waste, and studied the 5 Ss of organizing your home. You've discovered why it's important to broaden your skills through training in your areas of weakness, and learned how to make processes flow by minimizing interruptions so you can get in the zone. You've already seen a few examples, including:

- The laundry routine (Chapter 2)
- Taking out the trash (Chapter 4)
- Dishes (Chapter 7)
- Meal prep (Chapter 7)

Now you will step through a few more examples so you will feel confident about using these tools in your own life.

Working Out Example

Let's look at the process of working out. For Jamie, staying fit takes so much effort that she just can't stay motivated enough to keep up with it for very long. What if we identify the waste from the process and minimize the time commitment involved in working out? First, map out the process.

- Jamie puts on workout clothes. (10 min)
- She drives to the gym. (15 min)
- She participates in a one-hour workout class. (1 hr)
- She drives home. (15 min)
- She takes a shower. (20 min)

The entire process takes two hours out of her evening. As you look at this process, can you tell which of these steps add value to her life? First we need to look at what Jamie values. If we get to know her, we discover that working out isn't really a social activity for her. She is just going to the gym for the health benefits.

The workout itself is the only step that adds value. The shower doesn't add value on its own since she already takes a shower in the mornings too, but it is necessary if she works up a sweat. This is waste as over-processing, as well as wasted water if she is taking an extra shower after a workout. Let's see if there is a way she can get the same value without sacrificing so much time out of her evening.

How can she eliminate putting on workout clothes? This is waste as over-processing and movement. She can try sleeping in her workout clothes so they are already on when she wakes up.

Comfy clothes like yoga pants or sweats can do double duty as both PJs and workout clothes.

Let's come up with a way to eliminate the driving. There are at least two ways to do this. First, Jamie can find a gym near someplace else she already goes daily, like her workplace. This could eliminate or at least minimize the extra driving. Another solution to the non-value added step of driving to the gym is to find a workout program that she can do from home. YouTube has some great free workout channels. She may need some equipment for weight lifting, unless she decides to do something that doesn't require equipment like a cardio dance program. Another thing Jamie can do for a workout that doesn't require driving is to go for a run around the neighborhood.

Lastly, let's eliminate the shower. If she works out just before the time she would normally shower in the mornings then she does not have to add any extra showers to her workout days. This isn't possible if she has to drive to the gym and attend a one hour class (hence why she was trying to work out in the evenings). But if she can keep the rest of the process to just 45 minutes, Jamie thinks she can work out in the mornings before she showers and heads to school drop-off and goes to work.

Here's another way to look at this process. Realistically, she may not be willing to sacrifice more than 45 minutes of her day to staying fit if she is going to stick with it for the long haul. So she makes a routine for herself that fits within those time constraints and maximizes value to her. Forty-five minutes of solid workout time from home in the morning that she actually does consistently is much more effective than taking two hours of her evening to go to the gym, do a one hour class, and take an extra shower if she is less likely to stick to the latter routine.

Suddenly, staying fit doesn't seem like such a daunting task. Let's see the process now:

- Jamie sleeps in her t-shirt and sweatpants. (zero additional time)
- She does a 45 minute workout video in her living room.
- She showers at her usual time in the morning. (zero additional time)

Start to finish, the new process takes only 45 minutes so it's now possible for Jamie to do it in the morning before work. Because it doesn't consume two hours of the evening like it used to, Jamie is much more likely to stick with this routine. That's a win in her book.

Meal Planning Example

Diana is the type who looks at the clock, notices its 4:30 pm, and then asks "what can I whip up for dinner?" Then she looks through the pantry and freezer until brilliance hits her and she creates a mealtime miracle. Or more likely, she sees that she has most of the ingredients she needs for a recipe but she makes a quick run to the store to pick up the rest.

For this one we will take a different approach and design a meal-planning process from the ground up. Sometimes there may not be enough of a process to start with to try to break it down and rework it.

What are the things that add value to Diana's meal planning? Recipes and ingredients. These are the information and goods that make it possible for her to prepare a meal.

Diana has a few favorite recipes that her family likes even if she tries others on occasion, too. She typically brainstorms what she wants to make and then goes to look up the recipe.

Instead, Diana will keep her favorites in a folder. She will have another folder for recipes she would like to try from magazines or photocopied from books. This is the beginning of a system that will minimize searching through her inbox, stacks of papers, etc.

Next, she creates an inventory list of the pantry, fridge, and freezer as described in Chapter 4. She will always have a visual list to glance at and see what she has on hand so she won't have to go digging to see what is available to work with. She decides to keep one batch worth of the non-perishable ingredients from her favorite recipes on inventory and replace them when she uses them up.

Finally, she creates a visual system for planning her meals one week in advance. This will enable her to shop for ingredients

in one go and cut down on grocery trips. She does this using a meal planning board like the one shown.

This pretty and functional meal planning board helps her easily create a plan each week. Remember that folder where she decided to stash all her family's favorite recipes? She then wrote the names of the recipes on cut strips of index cards. This allows her to easily sort through a pile of recipe names and clip them next to the days she plans to make them. She also has strips that say "leftovers", "pizza", "eat out", and "new recipe" so she can cover the many types of meals she may want to account for. These strips of cardstock are stored in the pockets on the board and reused.

When it is time to plan the meals for the upcoming week she sorts through these little strips and plans out the meals based on the produce that is in season or the groceries she picked up that were on sale the week before. One grocery trip for all the missing items should be enough to set her up for the week. This eliminates the problem of lacking inspiration because she has all her favorites at her fingertips. She can also ensure that she is planning a variety of meals into the week when she sees it all laying out at once.

Emails Example

Many of us get overwhelmed by the sheer number of emails that come through each day. The process of visually scanning through fifty emails to find the five that actually contain valuable information is ridden with waste. Let's look at Jeanette's standard process for checking emails.

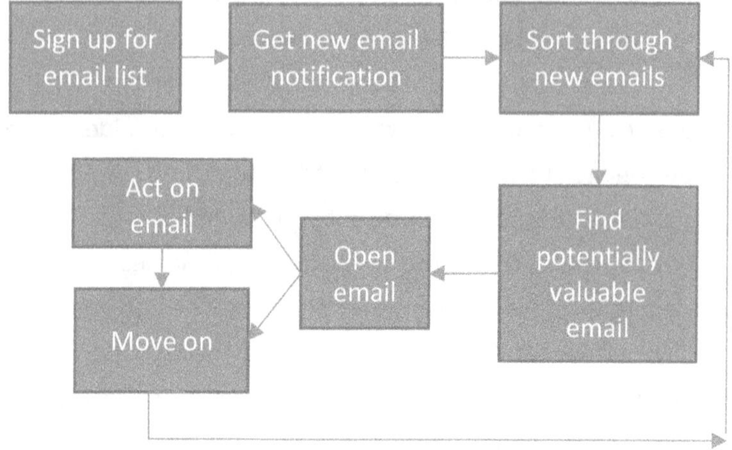

Jeanette spends more time searching for valuable emails than she does reading and acting on them once she finds them. If not for the fact that all of this clutter is electronic, this wouldn't be much different from sorting paper mail. Let's apply some of the Organization Strategies from Chapter 4 to make this process work better for Jeanette.

Sort and Systemize

For one week's time, Jeanette will look at all the emails that come in each day, and categorize (sort) and act on each of them a certain way (systemize).

Jeanette will classify every email that comes in by priority, and act according to what is written in the chart on the following page. The biggest offenders will stop coming to her inbox. She will soon find that the only emails she gets are emails she is interested in and a few sporadic ones she may have missed. Jeanette will have easy access to promotions she might be interested in when she chooses to look for them, but they won't be distracting her from the important, value adding messages.

She adopts the mindset that "less is more". Less junk emails in her inbox to sort through means more time freed up to act on the emails that add value to her life. She decides she'd rather err on the side of "less" because she can always re-subscribe to something she misses, though she probably won't even notice those emails are gone.

	Details	System
Never opens	These emails contain nothing she finds valuable. She has signed up for so many that she doesn't even open most because she doesn't shop at these places anymore or her shopping isn't dependent on what's in the ad.	These are a sort of low-hanging fruit and the easiest way to stop the inflow of these emails is to unsubscribe to each one as soon as it comes in.
Might open	She occasionally sees a subject line advertising something she was already looking for, but most of the time she skips right over them. Also, if she is going to visit a store anyway (online or in person) she might open up the advertisement first. Jeanette notices that these emails sometimes grab her attention in her inbox but they usually turn out to be a waste of her time. She would prefer to view them only when she was actually looking for something, instead of when the subject line snags her attention.	One solution for these is to create a filter that makes these emails skip the inbox and go straight to one "catch all" folder or to individual store folders. When she is specifically looking to visit one of these places she can easily peek at the latest emails in the folder.

Usually reads	She judges these by the subject line before reading them, but wants to see them in her inbox so she can have a chance to open them if they look intriguing.	These can be left as is and reassessed at a later date if she stops finding them interesting.
Always reads	This includes personal emails and her favorite blog subscriptions. These are the ones she actually wants to see in her inbox when she checks her email. If her inbox were full of these only, she would read every email that comes in.	She can leave these as is, or apply a filter that would highlight them to her so she reads them first.

Sanitize

Because she has a system in place, there shouldn't be much more cleaning involved.

If Jeanette isn't bothered by the thousands of past emails in her inbox it is ok for her not to go back and delete old ones. However, if they slow her down when she searches for things, they can easily be taken care of. She would first use a filter to sort out all from one email address. She then would delete them all at once using the "select all" button.

Jeanette will also sanitize by emptying out her spam folder. She quickly glances at them to make sure there aren't any important emails and then deletes them all.

Standardize and Sustain

Now that Jeanette has a process in place for unsubscribing from or filtering out unwanted emails, she decides to create an internal process to maintain her clutter-free inbox. First, she sees that the beginning of the process, when she signs up for emails, is when the clutter begins trickling in. If she is about to sign up for an email list, she will first ask herself, "Do I really think this will add value to my life? Is it conducive to achieving my broader goals?" Because she thinks twice about giving out her email address she can keep the tap shut on the flow of new junk emails.

After spending a week of thinking critically about EVERY email that comes in, Jeanette now is prone to noticing junk emails that are just taking up real estate at the top of her inbox. When she spots one of these types, she now acts on it immediately and unsubscribes or filters it to another folder without giving it a second thought. This is especially true about ones she has just recently subscribed to. She can quickly reassess their value once they start coming in. Because she did the hard work for a week, it has become second nature to her to think of her emails this way and the lean inbox is easy to maintain.

Sorting and Storing Receipts

Anthony believes it is important to save his receipts from every purchase. He isn't willing to budge on that. However, he loathes the process of sorting them chronologically and knows there must be a better way. He decides to map out this process by following the receipts through the value stream.

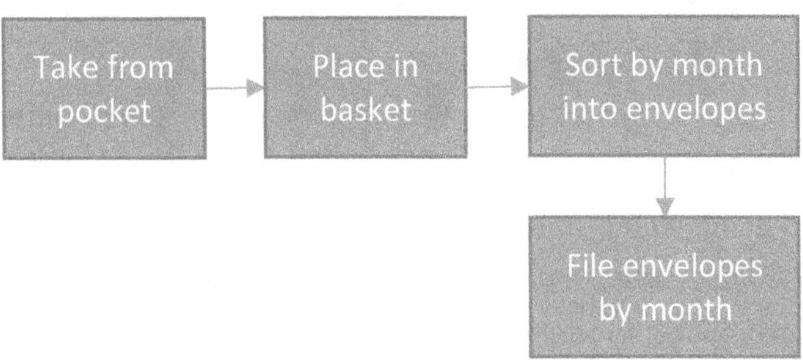

Anthony has been doing this process in this way for years now, and the sorting is so tedious that he can only bring himself to do it every six months or so when he can't fit another single receipt in the basket. He wishes there were a way to not have to spend so much time on this process and still get the benefit of having his receipts neatly organized by month.

Anthony looks at the process to assess which steps add value. He knows the receipts have to go in his pocket first. He likes collecting them in a basket so he can empty his pockets into one spot with little thinking required. The sorting part doesn't exactly add value but it might be necessary to getting them organized unless he can find another way. Lastly, putting the envelopes in the filing cabinet in chronological order is a small and necessary step but it doesn't add value.

Anthony recognizes that the six-month accumulation of receipts is his biggest problem. He does a root cause analysis by asking "Why?" until he can get to the source of the problem.

"Why does it take so long to sort the receipts?"

"Because there are so many in there."

"Why does the basket get so full?"

"Because they collect there for months and get all mixed up."

"Why do they get all mixed up?"

"Because more than one month's receipts accumulate in there before it gets emptied."

This is when it dawns on him. The receipts aren't placed in the basket all mixed up. When the basket is freshly sorted and emptied, all receipts that go in there are from the same month. As soon as a new month starts and he puts more receipts in there, the basket will require sorting. What if he empties the basket into a new envelope on the first of every month? They never get mixed up, and the sorting step is completely eliminated.

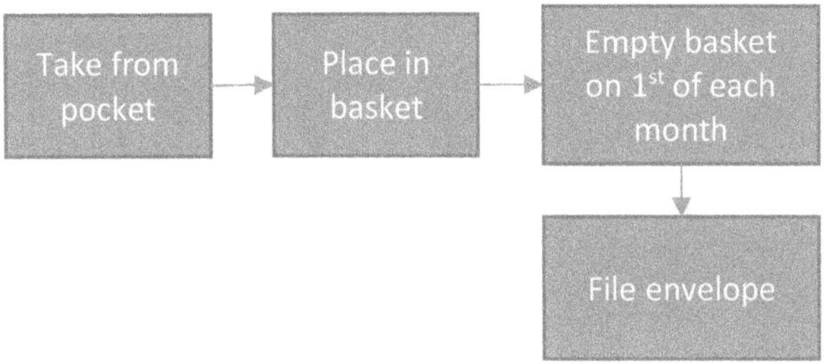

Anthony tries this and is blown away that he doesn't have to sort EVER again, as long as he is diligent to empty the basket at the beginning of every month into a new envelope. He also files this envelope immediately into the place where he keeps all the previous months. Anthony is so glad he re-thought how he was handling these receipts because he has completely eliminated the task he dreads the most!

Are you feeling encouraged yet? There is no task too big or small to improve. In each of these examples, someone intimately involved in the process (who stands the most to gain from its improvement) has stood back, looked at it from a different perspective, and used a few simple tools to make some drastic improvements. There is no right or wrong way to do a process, but there is always room to improve it and make it better fit the needs of those impacted by it.

9

Toolbox and Launchpad

As you've been reading thus far you have probably thought of some tasks and processes in your own life that could use a remodel. If you've already started redesigning those, great! Keep at it. If not, keep reading on to gain the confidence you need to get moving.

Review

Let's review the tools in your tool belt.

Defining Value

Before you can remove waste from a process, you have to identify what it is you and the people you serve actually want from the process. Who is the customer and what do they value? Why do you do this process?

Identifying the 7 Types of Waste

Rework- when things don't turn out right the first time.

Overproduction- making more than you need.

Over-processing- things being too complicated.

Motion- people going from one place to another.

Transport- carrying things from one place to another.

Waiting- waiting for one step to finish before you can move on to another.

Inventory- storing things that may become obsolete or may expire before use.

Organizing with the 5 S's

Sort: Separate useful items from unnecessary ones. Then sort by parts, tools, and instructions.

Systemize: Give everything a place, and put everything in its place.

Sanitize: Dust, sweep, scrub, and shine all of your living and storage space. Cleanliness reveals problems.

Standardize: Create standardized processes for routine cleaning and regular maintenance.

Sustain: Routinely perform root cause analysis. Ask "why?". Stick to standard work processes. Keep learning and improving.

Using Visual Cues

These can include:

- visible storage in profile view,
- color coding to make things easy to find and minimize errors,
- labeling appropriately for the users,
- making important information easily accessible and clearly visible,
- visual indicators to signal when to take an action,

- visual logs to track performance and problems,
- graphical charts for kids,
- moving an item or marker when task is completed, and
- monitoring the status of tasks.

Gaining Skills

Sometimes you can't improve a task or process any further until you get some additional training. Don't let an awareness of your natural gifting keep you from learning other things that are harder for you.

Have a growth mindset and believe that you can learn more than your natural gifting.

Flow and the Experience of Work

Map the value stream: Draw a diagram of how materials and information flow in a process.

Improve flow: Minimize the time spent waiting for previous steps to be completed.

Minimize interruptions: Anticipate common interruptions (like phones and children) and try to mitigate them beforehand. For those that can't be prevented or planned for, address them quickly as they come up and get back to the task at hand.

Now Try Your Own!

Pick a process:

____

Identify what you (or those you serve) value in the process. What is the "customer" actually looking for?

____

____

____

Diagram your process by mapping the value stream:

Which steps add value?

____

Which steps do not add value but are necessary for now?

____

Which steps are waste?
Rework

____

Overproduction

____

Over-processing

____

Motion

____

Transport

____

Waiting

____

Inventory

____

Perform root cause analysis of tough problems, if necessary:

Problem____
Why?

____

Why?

____

Why?

____

Why?

____

Why?

____

Re-design the process.
Diagram the new process:

Try your improved process.
Keep fine tuning and making adjustments as necessary. Pursue perfection.

10

Big Picture Domestic Engineering

Are you starting to catch on to this concept of Domestic Engineering? Instead of letting your to-do list overwhelm you, if you have re-engineered some of the processes in your home life, you may have seen your work load lighten up a bit as tasks have become simpler, quicker, and less wasteful. Don't stop there!

Expand Your Horizons.

At the core of Domestic Engineering is the question, "What do I value?" Remember when you defined those in Chapter 2? Flip back there now and remind yourself of what's really important to you.

Now take a step back from the tasks in your home, and look at your day as one very BIG process. You have many things scheduled and some unplanned or unscheduled activities that fill in the gaps. Consider each of these activities as it relates to the question, "Does this add value to my life?"

One way to start looking at the process of your day is to begin by documenting everything you do in a week. Your planner or calendar would be a great starting place, but don't forget to record tasks that aren't appointments, too.

As you look at the things on your plate over a couple weeks' time you will notice that there will be activities that you do out of habit, but when you really stop to think of their value, you don't see any. Here are a few examples:

Social Groups

Jenna has three different social groups she meets with each week: a church fellowship group, a women's Bible study, and a mom's meetup/play group. While she enjoys all of them, she sees many of the same women and kids at the playdate as she does at the women's Bible study. Childcare is provided at the women's group so her kids play with the same kids as they do at their play group. Jenna assesses whether all of these weekly meetings are necessary and valuable to her family. She realizes that she could cut out the mom's meetup/play group because it doesn't add significant value to her or her kids, and it utilizes an entire morning every week that she could use for a different activity. She decides to cut it out of her schedule, and realizes that she doesn't really miss it (and neither do her kids).

A Digital Addiction

Yvetta (hey, that's me!) checks her phone frequently. She checks for new emails and texts, scrolls through Facebook, and looks things up on the web when the notion strikes her. While she occasionally discovers things of value there, the amount of valuable information she gathers is not congruent to the amount of times she checks her phone in a day. She and her husband personally value keeping the kids away from screens as much as possible, so Yvetta feels a little guilty when she is on the phone a lot in front of her kids. It's a tempting habit that's hard to kick but she knows it's taking away from what she really values- spending intentional time with her kids. Yvetta feels it would be beneficial to check her phone less often, although she would have to overcome the temptation by leaving it out of arms reach. She has an idea: she will place her phone in a designated holding basket away from where she typically sits in whichever room she is in at home. When it alerts her of a new email or text, she can go to it and check it, respond, and then return it to the basket. She tries this and finds that she is less tempted to jump on it all the time because it's less convenient to do so. While this has added the small extra steps of putting it in a basket and retrieving it, in the long run this will save her much wasted time.

Grocery Shopping

Yvetta (me again!) makes a weekly trip to a particular grocery store that has overlapping ads on Wednesdays. Every Wednesday, the store's ad for the previous week, as well as the ad for the next week, are both valid. Because twice as many things are on sale, Yvetta shops on Wednesdays to stock up on produce for the week. However, the grocery store is a 20 minute drive from her house. She also notices that her family doesn't finish the produce before it goes bad. She realizes that she can get the same benefit (and not miss anything that goes on sale) if she goes every other week and shops from both ads. By doing this she saves herself a 1 ½ hour outing to the store every other week and wastes less produce that way. There was no value to going every week so she nixed it, and she's glad she did!

Carving Out "Me Time"

Lauren has two kids under two, and she finds it challenging to get any time to herself on most days. Before her second little one was born, she used to savor a little "me" time in the quiet moments when her child napped. She really *values* that time. Now with her older child taking one long nap in the afternoon and her baby taking two sporadic naps in a day, she doesn't get any quiet time to herself unless their naps happen to overlap. And even then, she usually is so behind on chores that by the time she sits down, one of the children is waking up.

Because that "me" time is so valuable to Lauren, she decides to try some things to make overlapping naps a more consistent feature in her day. First, she takes a look at the days where the naptime coincidentally overlapped and tries to figure out what factors contributed to this small miracle. Lauren soon starts to notice patterns in her little one's routine, and she tests out her hypotheses. She discovers she can keep her baby up just a tad longer before her second nap while she puts the oldest to bed and then put them both down to nap at the same time. Lauren is finally able to get some much needed time to herself!

However, she has a tendency to immediately start cleaning up the house or cooking dinner because it's so much easier to do those things alone. She decides that her "me" time is her first priority when the naptimes align, so she focuses on getting more of those chores done, albeit very slowly, while the kids are awake. She gives herself permission to drop whatever chores are in progress and put them on hold until the kids wake up. She has more patience and energy for her kids and chores if she gets that time to recharge her own batteries first.

What Would Add Value to My Life?

When you took the time to define what you value in Chapter 2, you may have discovered that there are things you value that aren't a part of your life right now. Whether or not that's true for you, here is an exercise for you. Imagine it's the end of the year and you are reflecting on what you've done with those past 365 days. What activities, tasks, and accomplishments would make you satisfied to think about? Or another way of looking at it is this – ask yourself, "what would *add* value to my life?" You might have a few things that jump out at you. Are there places you'd like to visit? Do you have dreams and goals you'd like to accomplish? Are there friends you'd like to get together with? Things you'd like to learn? What would *add* value to your life?

You may be familiar with the concept of a bucket list. It's a list of things you'd like to check off before you die. What if you make a list in a similar fashion, but with a shorter time frame, like, say, three months? Pack it full of dreams, goals, places, and activities that you realistically would like to check off in the next three months. Get the whole family involved in crafting the list and then carrying it through. It's a way of holding yourselves accountable to have fun and live intentionally! You are prioritizing the things that really make your family come alive. A year well-planned is a year well-lived. Write it down, and then go after it! You will be so glad you did.

11

A Culture of Improvement

By now you may have tackled a few processes already and seen some things starting to improve in your day to day life. Keep it up. The more you start applying these strategies, the more they become second nature. Instead of looking at a frustrating chore and thinking "this stinks!" your thought will be "how can I make this better?"

Now that you have a tool belt full of skills and tools to help you eliminate waste from your day to day life, you don't have to limit improvements to major problem areas. Waiting for big problems to come up is not as effective as keeping an eye out for small issues and areas of waste and then tackling them expediently.

Keeping an Eye Out for Problems

Remember those 7 types of waste? Let's look at some of the warning signs.

Type of Waste	Associated Phrases	Other Signs
Rework	"Oops!" "Let's try this again." "I should have asked first."	It was done incorrectly.
Overproduction	"I thought you'd like this so I made a double batch." "I'll get this ready just in case."	Throwing out/giving away extras you have made.
Over-processing	"Am I doing this right?" "How did I do this last time?"	It's complicated. Lots of steps. Hard for others to do it correctly.
Transport	"It's over there." "Let me go get that." "Let me find that."	Making extra trips to grab something.
Waiting	"I have some downtime." "Let's leave these here while we…"	Getting distracted with something else. Timers. Process takes a long time.
Motion	"I'll be right there!" "My arm is getting tired."	Switching between tasks in different places.

		Tired, achy body.
Inventory	"I know it's here somewhere." "I stocked up on a great deal!" "Now, where did I put that?" "I must have something here for that."	Clutter. Overflowing storage areas. Throwing away things that have become obsolete or passed expiration dates. Much sorting to find what you want.

Put on your "waste lenses" as you are going about your day, and develop a culture of stopping to fix problems as you notice them. If you have a tendency to create workarounds for things that aren't happening efficiently, stop and revisit the original problem. Doing so could save you a lot of time in the long run. Do a root cause analysis to uncover the real problem when it's not immediately obvious.

When you notice waste (remember, this is anything that uses resources but doesn't add value), you may try to fix it and realize the problem is still there. Or, you may have created waste in another form. Don't be discouraged. Keep trying solutions until you find the way that works best. Do you think that ingenuity always happens on the first try? Probably not. Great minds like the Wright Brothers and Alexander Graham Bell experimented, tweaked, and perfected things over and over before they created the inventions they were known for. And even after that, the inventions they created have morphed and adapted with every new relevant scientific advancement.

Sometimes we have been doing something one way for so long that we can't see any other way of doing it. While you may be the expert in the things you do every day, you may also be blind to the inefficiencies in it. Bring in a fresh pair of eyes. Consult your spouse, or a friend, or an owner's manual, or even a blog or YouTube video. Observe how others accomplish something, and see if there is something you can apply to help you do it better.

When new tasks are introduced into your life, or you experience major life changes like a move, a change of season or employment, or a kid going off to school, it is an opportune time to revisit any processes that may be affected by these changes.

For example, you might be in the habit of cooking certain meals, and cleaning the house quite frequently. Then your last teenager goes off to college and the house is rather quiet. If you take this major life change as an opportunity to rework some of your habits, you might realize you can start making foods that you and your spouse prefer and cooking less often instead of catering to your teenager's eating habits. You also might notice that the second bathroom doesn't have to be cleaned every week. You were in the habit of running the dishwasher every night because it always seemed to be full. But now, with only two in the house, you find that every other day is sufficient.

If you take the time to notice these things, particularly after you experience a major change to your routines and habits, you can take full advantage of removing waste from things that were once necessary steps under different circumstances.

When you move, you have an opportunity to design your home life afresh with the new factors taken into consideration. Design your routines and habits from the ground up in a way that makes sense with your new surroundings and needs using lean principles from the beginning. It is far easier to start there and engineer your home life in a waste-free way from the beginning than it is to try to redo processes once you've been doing them for a while. You are learning new routines anyway in your new environment, so why not make them value-centered right from the get-go?

Lean living is contagious. You start tackling projects and processes in your home and it's hard not to share with others what you're discovering. Every improvement is a small victory that makes room for more of what you value in your life. Let this prompt a dialogue between you and your biggest customers—your family.

Have you taken the time yet to talk with them about what you all actually want and value in your family life? Ask the most important people in your life where they would like to see improvements in their home environment. Ask them if you are meeting your responsibilities to them. Little ones may not be able to answer these questions but you can often judge from their behavior whether or not their needs are being met. Involve them not only in measuring the success of the processes but in engineering them as well. Train every little pair of eyes (and big ones too!) to spot waste. If you narrate your thought process when you notice waste they will catch on.

Last year I bought a castle pop-up tent for my two year old because I thought it was the coolest thing ever. She already had a smaller tent with characters on it, but it was not nearly as exciting, in my opinion. I set up the castle for her downstairs while she napped. When she came down the stairs she saw it and said, "Mommy, why did you buy that? I already have one." My two year old called me out on my materialistic tendencies. While I was a little bit ashamed of my poor judgement, I was simultaneously proud that my little one was learning to spot waste. She had heard me say to her in the store many times, in many situations, "we don't need that, we already have one at home," and she took it to heart. This experience made me realize that she is always watching and listening. She may not know what is going on in my head, but if I think out loud in front of her, her impressionable little mind is going to start thinking the same way. And hey, if all five of us can learn to spot waste and improve processes, there will be five heads working on the same problems. The creative problem-solving potential will be exponential!

Stop Benchmarking

When you start running with all these lean ideas you may have a tendency to look at what others are doing and start comparing. This is dangerous. Don't do it. To try ideas and solutions from other people is ok and can even be beneficial. But don't use their results as a benchmark to measure your level of success.

When you compare, there are two possible outcomes and neither one is good. Let's say you compare the cleanliness of your home to that of your friend Sally's home. If you see that her house looks cleaner than yours, you will probably feel inadequate and try to copy what she is doing. However, you don't have the same situation as she does and there are a lot of factors you aren't seeing that contribute to the house being perceived as clean.

Using her home as a benchmark for measuring the cleanliness of your own home might be futile when you consider factors like the age of her home (everything looks newer and cleaner to begin with), the number of small children in the household, the wood and tile floors vs. carpet, number and types of pets, and whether either of you works outside the home. Also, Sally's clean home might appear clutter-free but it may not actually be sanitary. Or, Sally's home might be clean because she spent two days cleaning like a crazy woman before she had company over. If you try to hold yourself to the standard you see in her home, you may get frustrated when you find it just doesn't work for you in *your* home with *your* family and *your* lifestyle.

On the other hand, if you compare your home to Sally's and you believe that yours is cleaner, you are likely to conclude that you don't have anything to improve on. Maybe you had ambitiously been planning to clean the baseboards this week. You noticed some dust on hers and began to second guess yourself. You rationalized not cleaning yours because it's not that important if Sally's baseboards didn't look clean. Instead of trying to improve your own situation you took an attitude of lazy contentment. You chose not to do what was best for your own home (despite previous good intentions) because you played the comparison game and came out on top.

In either case, the outcome was not good.

Think of Domestic Engineering as a race. If you look to the lanes to the right and to the left while running, you are likely to swerve. If you look at the finish line and focus on achieving *your* personal best, you will put all your energy into running forward.

The Termites Undermining Your Progress

There are a few pesky little enemies to this culture of improvement you desire for your home. Keep an eye out for these villains:

- A fixed mindset that says you'll never be good at something, so why even try?
- The belief that there is only one right way of doing a task.
- Unwillingness to listen to other ideas.
- Poor communication of changes in the process to those involved.
- Closed ears that don't want to hear feedback.
- Lack of team participation.
- A belief that you have already achieved perfection.

Press on Toward Perfection

Look for waste. Pick the low-hanging fruit first. Enjoy the significant improvements that come with minimal effort. Relish in the quicker, leaner processes that make more room in your life for what you value most. Then start shaking those branches that are just out of reach – the steps that don't add value but are necessary. And then, when you think you've got it just right, climb higher. Keep fine-tuning. Revisit the processes when circumstances and needs change. Pursue perfection. There is no such thing as perfection, but there is always something more perfect to pursue.

How far have you come? Have you remodeled your home life to make room for what you really value? If you jumped in with two feet then you're probably reaping the benefits of a simpler, less wasteful life already. You spend less time just trying to keep up. You aren't trying to be here and there and everywhere. You are sensitive to notice tasks that are burning your time, energy, brainpower, space, and resources. You see when something needs to change and you do it on the spot. You have banished unnecessary inventory, and changed how you shop, freeing up real estate in your home. You keep track of what needs to be done and how things are progressing, and have mastered the art and science of turning the evidence into positive changes to your systems, both big and small.

Congratulations! You are the engineer of your home life. Instead of letting your life just happen, you intentionally tell every process and every task how it should work for you, and then you do it! You aren't afraid to try new, unconventional things to make your life easier. You have more time to spend on the people and things you love. You are a domestic engineer. Keep building the life you love.

Appendix

List of Examples

- The Laundry Routine (Chapter 2)
- Taking Out the Trash (Chapter 4)
- Inventory Management (Chapter 4)
- Dishes (Chapter 7)
- Meal Prep (Chapter 7)
- Working Out (Chapter 8)
- Meal Planning (Chapter 8)
- Emails (Chapter 8)
- Receipts (Chapter 8)
- Social Groups (Chapter 10)
- Digital Addiction (Chapter 10)
- Grocery Shopping (Chapter 10)
- Carving Out "Me Time" (Chapter 10)
- Clean House Comparison (Chapter 11)

More resources and tools can be found at:

www.more-than-rubies.com/LifestyleRedesigned

If you have a question, or a process you'd like me to feature on my blog, email me at: MoreThanRubiesYvetta@gmail.com

Process:

Identify what you (or those you serve) value in the process. What is the "customer" actually looking for?

____

____

____

Diagram your process by mapping the value stream:

Which steps add value?

____

Which steps do not add value but are necessary for now?

____

Which steps are waste?
Rework

____

Overproduction

____

Over-processing

____

Motion

____

Transport

____

Waiting

____

Inventory

____

Perform root cause analysis of tough problems, if necessary:

Problem:_______________________________________

Why?

____

Why?

____

Why?

____

Why?

____

Why?

____

Re-design the process.
Diagram the new process:

Try your improved process.
Keep fine tuning and making adjustments as necessary. Pursue perfection!

Process Name:

____

Identify what you (or those you serve) value in the process. What is the "customer" actually looking for?

____

____

____

Diagram your process by mapping the value stream:

Which steps add value?

____

Which steps do not add value but are necessary for now?

____

Which steps are waste?
Rework

____

Overproduction

____

Over-processing

____

Motion

____

Transport

____

Waiting

____

Inventory

____

Perform root cause analysis of tough problems, if necessary:

Problem:____
Why?

____

Why?

____

Why?

____

Why?

____

Why?

____

Re-design the process.

Diagram the new process:

Try your improved process.

Keep fine tuning and making adjustments as necessary. Pursue perfection!

Process Name:

____

Identify what you (or those you serve) value in the process. What is the "customer" actually looking for?

____

____

____

Diagram your process by mapping the value stream:

Which steps add value?

____

Which steps do not add value but are necessary for now?

____

Which steps are waste?
Rework

____

Overproduction

____

Over-processing

____

Motion

____

Transport

____

Waiting

____

Inventory

____

Perform root cause analysis of tough problems, if necessary:

Problem:____
Why?

____

Why?

____

Why?

____

Why?

____

Why?

____

Re-design the process.
Diagram the new process:

Try your improved process.
Keep fine tuning and making adjustments as necessary. Pursue
perfection!

Process Name:

____

Identify what you (or those you serve) value in the process. What is the "customer" actually looking for?

____

____

____

Diagram your process by mapping the value stream:

Which steps add value?

____

Which steps do not add value but are necessary for now?

____

Which steps are waste?
Rework

____

Overproduction

____

Over-processing

____

Motion

____

Transport

____

Waiting

____

Inventory

____

Perform root cause analysis of tough problems, if necessary:

Problem:_______________________________________

Why?

____

Why?

____

Why?

____

Why?

____

Why?

____

Re-design the process.

Diagram the new process:

Try your improved process.

Keep fine tuning and making adjustments as necessary. Pursue perfection!

Bibliography

Baumeister, Roy F., and John Tierney. *Willpower: Rediscovering the Greatest Human Strength*. New York, NY: Penguin Books, 2012.

Cilley, Marla. *Sink Reflections*. New York: Bantam Books, 2004.

Dweck, Carol S. *Mindset: the New Psychology of Success*. New York: Ballantine Books, 2016.

Kondo, Marie, and Cathy Hirano. *The Life-Changing Magic of Tidying Up*. London: Vermilion, 2014.

Womack, James P., Daniel T. Jones, and Daniel Roos. *The Machine That Changed the World: the Story of Lean Production - Toyotas Secret Weapon in the Global Car Wars That Is Revolutionizing World Industry*. London: Simon & Schuster, 2007.

Womack, James P., and Daniel T. Jones. *Lean Thinking: Banish Waste and Create Wealth in Your Corporation*. New York: Free Press, 2003.

www.ingramcontent.com/pod-product-compliance
Lightning Source LLC
Chambersburg PA
CBHW061543050726
47593CB00002B/884